holy scriptures" 2 Tim 3:15

Charles Haddon Spurgeon

Who is the Greatest?

The true story of
Charles Haddon Spurgeon and his
gospel preaching

Catherine Mackenzie
Illustrated by Rita Ammassari

Young Charles felt so cold. His fingers and feet hurt as he trudged through the snow. His nose was like a block of ice. He decided to go inside a nearby church to get warm. Charles Spurgeon wasn't famous, he wasn't a great name, but this sixteen-year-old was about to have his life changed for ever. The year was 1850.

Young Charles felt so cold.

Charles sat down on one of the old wooden seats. A preacher was reading from the Bible. Towards the end of the sermon he turned to Charles and called out loudly, 'Young man,' the Lord says, 'Look unto me and be ye saved.'

That Bible verse was Isaiah 45:22 – and when Spurgeon heard it he looked to Jesus Christ for salvation. Charles knew he was a great sinner, and that Jesus was the only one who could save him from his sin.

Charles knew he was a great sinner.

Some weeks later Charles was baptized in the River Lark. He knew that God wanted him to be a preacher. He gave his very first sermon in a little cottage in the village of Taversham. Dressed in waterproof clothes he walked across the fields with a lantern to preach to the country folk. Preaching would be part of Spurgeon's life from that day on. Charles knew that without the one true salvation from Jesus Christ, all are lost with no hope of heaven. Charles knew that Jesus was the only hope.

Charles knew that Jesus was the only hope.

Soon Charles was asked to become the minister at New Park Street chapel. The congregation was small at first but grew – a lot! Charles preached from the Bible in a way that ordinary people could understand. He even acted out Bible passages and would pace back and fore dramatically. His enemies described him as 'the preaching buffoon', but Spurgeon didn't care. He said, 'I must and will make people listen.' More and more people came to hear Charles. Soon the church was overflowing. They had to move to another building.

More and more people came to hear Charles.

When he was in his twenties, Charles got married to a young woman named Susannah. They began working for God together. Charles preached and wrote. Susannah looked after their two boys and began a charity to help preachers obtain good Christian books. The interest in Charles' preaching spread. His sermons were translated into nearly forty languages. Spurgeon was a great preacher, but he knew that it was God who was behind this. It was God who made Spurgeon great.

Charles got married to a young woman named Susannah.

There were problems though. The congregation was so big it had to move into the large Surrey Music Hall. One night someone decided to pretend that a fire had started. The congregation stampeded out of the building. Several people died in the crush. The terrible event affected Spurgeon deeply. For many years his emotions would get the better of him. Charles would often burst into tears.

Charles would often burst into tears.

Spurgeon's work continued, however. Colleges were founded, charities started, and books were published. Throughout his life, at least 135 of his books and pamphlets were printed, yet preaching was the important work. In his lifetime he preached nearly 3,600 sermons. Sometimes he preached to thousands, but then sometimes to just one.

Sometimes he preached to thousands.

One day Charles was going to preach in a new venue. He wanted to find out if his voice would carry across the hall, so he went down early and called out in a loud voice, 'Behold the Lamb of God which taketh away the sin of the world.' A carpenter was working late. The man heard the Bible verse, packed away his tools and went home. There he knelt down, prayed and believed in Jesus.

Charles went on to preach to hundreds of more people. But it was always the good news of Jesus Christ no matter how many heard it.

It was always the good news of Jesus Christ.

The time came for Spurgeon's congregation to have a building of their own. The Metropolitan Tabernacle was built in 1861. The church was big enough to sit five thousand people. Spurgeon donated a lot of his own money to the building fund. You can visit the Metropolitan Tabernacle in London today.

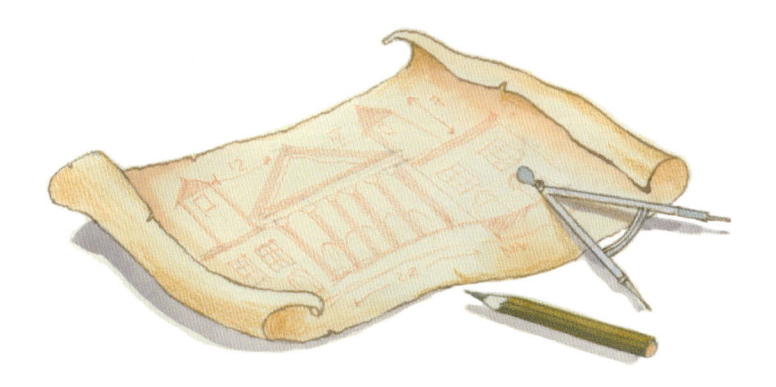

The church was big enough to sit five thousand people.

Another problem Spurgeon had, was with people who didn't believe the Bible. They said it wasn't the Word of God. These people didn't believe that Jesus died so that sinners could be saved from eternal punishment. Spurgeon accused them of downgrading the Bible. He strongly disagreed with them.

Mrs Spurgeon became very ill and could no longer attend church. Charles got sick too. His doctors told him to take a holiday. So he visited the South of France because there is better weather there. However, on 31st January 1892, while he was in Mentone in France, Charles Spurgeon died.

His doctors told him to take a holiday.

Thousands of people walked past his coffin in the days before his funeral. Many of them must have remembered his preaching. Often Charles encouraged people to look to Jesus for comfort and help.

Spurgeon said that a good character is the best tombstone. Those who loved you and were helped by you will remember you when forget-me-nots have withered. Carve your name on hearts, not on marble.

When the time comes for you to die, you need not be afraid, because death cannot separate you from God's love.

Death cannot separate you from God's love.

With thanks to God for faithful preachers and their message throughout my life.

Copyright © 2019 Catherine Mackenzie
ISBN: 978-1-5271-0393-1

Published by Christian Focus Publications
Geanies House, Fearn, Tain, Ross-shire, IV20 1TW,
Scotland, U.K.
www.christianfocus.com

Scripture quotations are based on the King James Version

Cover design by Daniel van Straaten
Illustrated by Rita Ammassari
Printed in China